Life in Extremes

Contents

T0328012

Written by Danny Pearson

Collins

1 Life in extremes

How have people adapted to live in places so hot that you have to live underground to hide from the sun? How do people thrive in places so cold that your eyelashes freeze together? Do you know where the hottest and coldest places are on the planet?

We're going to discover how people live in some of the world's most extreme climates. How do they adapt to their surroundings? How do they find food and what do they do to make their lives more comfortable?

2 Where are the coldest places?

Imagine living somewhere so cold that your eyelashes freeze together. How would you adapt to life there?

Oymyakon, Russia, is the coldest **inhabited** place on Earth. Once the temperature there was recorded at –71.2 degrees Celsius.

Fact!

Car engines can freeze so quickly that some people keep car engines running at all times.

Around 500 people live here. Water moves at high temperatures to avoid pipes freezing. The locals melt blocks of ice inside their homes for fresh water.

Crops can't grow here because the land is permanently frozen. Local people eat mostly fish, reindeer and horse, which is sometimes eaten frozen.

If the temperature drops below −55 degrees Celsius, then children can stay home from school. How would freezing cold temperatures like this affect your life?

Fact!

The temperature of a normal kitchen freezer is around −18 degrees Celsius.

Utqiagvik is a **remote** Alaskan town. On one side of the town is a huge **tundra**, and on the other side is the Arctic Ocean, which is frozen for most of the year.

Just over 4,000 people live here. The city is reachable only by aircraft or by sea. During the summer months, when the Arctic Ocean unfreezes, boats can reach Utqiagvik carrying large goods that can't fit on planes.

The town is in almost complete darkness from November until January, and summer temperatures reach just above freezing. It's tough living in Utqiaġvik, but the wildlife is breathtaking. Polar bears, walruses, seals and reindeer are some of the animals that can be spotted here.

Some cities have gone to extreme lengths to keep people protected during the cold winters.

The Chicago Pedway, USA, stretches underground for about eight kilometres through the city centre. It's a system of underground tunnels and overhead bridges. Thousands of people use the Pedway every day. The whole system connects over 50 buildings.

The Pedway offers shelter from the city's extremely cold winters. It also reduces the amount of traffic and pollution. What other things might help people to survive in such cold temperatures?

Fact!

The PATH network in Toronto, Canada, is the largest underground shopping centre in the world.

Where's the coldest place you've been?

Ulaanbaatar, Mongolia, is 1,350 metres above sea level. On average, it's the coldest capital city in the world. The average annual temperature is around –2 degrees Celsius.

Mongolia is a huge country but it's mainly rural. Half the population live in cities and some are **nomadic**.

Mongolian **herders** need to lead their animals to find better areas to feed. They live in gers (meaning "home"). Gers are round tents covered with felt made from thick sheep's wool.

Gers allow the herders to move and live comfortably throughout the year in Mongolia's extreme climate. The temperature varies between −40 degrees Celsius in the winter and +40 degrees Celsius in the summer.

inside a modern-day ger

Fact!

Mongolia is also known as "the land of the blue sky", as it has over 260 days of clear, blue sky per year.

11

Closer look
Inuit

CANADA

The Inuit are nomadic people who have adapted to the extreme cold of the Arctic regions of Greenland, Canada and Alaska. They are famous for their survival and hunting skills.

People can't grow crops due to the millions of square kilometres of ice and tundra being permanently frozen.

Early Inuit people were skilled hunters and could catch food all year round. Winter homes were made from snow and ice. The Inuit word for this temporary home is "igloo". In the summer, the Inuit made their homes from animal skin stretched over driftwood or whale bones. How did these two different building methods help to cope with the different seasons?

Most modern-day Inuit people live in permanent houses with electricity and heating. However, the hunting culture and skills are still very much a part of the Inuit way of life.

3 Living in the dark

Rjukan, Norway, is known as one of the darkest towns on Earth. It has no direct sunlight from September to March because of the surrounding mountains.

The locals installed giant mirrors on the mountains, 450 metres above the town. These mirrors track the movement of the sun across the town and reflect some much-needed sunlight onto the town square.

One local said, "This is so warming. Not just physically, but mentally. It's mentally warming."

4 Where are the hottest places?

How would you deal with the heat if you lived in the hottest place on Earth?

Welcome to the driest, lowest and hottest region in North America. Death Valley, USA, holds the world record for the highest air temperature of 56.7 degrees Celsius. That was recorded in 1913.

One local said, "When you walk outside, it's like walking into an oven; you don't feel yourself sweat because it evaporates so quickly."

Fact!

There is less than five centimetres of rain in Death Valley every year.

Most homes have powerful air-conditioning units that take in the hot air and filter it through wet pads to cool it down. People usually exercise at night in the slightly cooler temperatures.

Even though it's extremely hot, the park is home to about 1,000 plant species and over 400 kinds of animals that have adapted to this harsh desert environment.

What sorts of plants and animals do you think would survive in this heat?

Around 2,000 people live in Coober Pedy, Australia. Over half of the population live in below-ground residences called "dugouts". These have been built to avoid the scorching summer daytime heat of around 36.7 degrees Celsius.

The dugouts are huge. There's even an underground campsite where people can pitch their tents.

There's a golf course above ground, where locals play games at night with glow-in-the-dark golf balls. Why do you think they play golf at night?

the entrance to the dugouts

These underground homes were also built to escape the uncomfortable daytime heat. They are in Matmata, Tunisia.

Doha, Qatar, is so hot that the city has air-conditioning at its outdoor shopping centres. This is to protect people from the summer temperatures which can reach a sweltering 46 degrees Celsius.

One of the busiest roads there, near one of the city's biggest markets, was painted blue. It helps to lower the temperature as dark coloured roads absorb more heat from the sun than lighter roads, which reflect it.

Local football fans, and players, can keep cool as they have even installed air-conditioning in their football stadiums.

Las Vegas, USA, is in the hot Nevada desert. To beat the heat, people are cooled by mist sprayers which are installed along the main streets.

Death Valley, Doha and Las Vegas are hot but none of them are as hot as Dallol, Ethiopia.

It has the highest average temperature of any place on the planet.

No one lives in Dallol full-time, but it is regularly visited by tourists and scientists. They are attracted to this area for its outstanding landscapes. The area is covered with **geysers** and acid ponds. You can hike up to the crater of Erta Ale, an active volcano that's home to a lava lake.

One scientist who worked there said, "On average, the temperature around lunchtime can reach 48 degrees Celsius. One time we measured 55 degrees Celsius."

23

Closer look
Tuareg people

Tuareg people have adapted to extreme heat over thousands of years.

Around two million Tuareg live around the Sahara Desert. Tuareg men traditionally wear dark blue clothes with a piece of clothing called the "tagelmust": an indigo-blue turban with a veil. What do you think the benefits of this are?

The tagelmust protects people from the sun, and the sand blown up by the desert winds. Darker clothes absorb more sunlight and heat radiated from the body than white clothes.

Most Tuareg today have several jobs which include farming, trading and herding. They use camels to travel vast distances over desert plains, grasslands and volcanic mountain ranges.

Fact!

Tuareg people are sometimes known as "the blue people of the Sahara". This is due to the blue dye, used to colour the cloth, staining their skin.

5 Do people live near volcanoes?

Reykjavik, Iceland, is the world's most northerly capital. It has a population of just over 130,000 people that are under constant threat from volcanic activity and earthquakes.

The heat created by the volcanic activity on this island is used to help create electricity.

How would you feel living next to a volcano?

Fact!

Iceland is the fourth happiest country in the world, according to the World Happiness Report.

The town of Heimaey in Iceland sits at the bottom of the Eldfell volcano.

Hawai'i Volcanoes National Park, USA, is one of the few places in the world where you can come close to an active volcano.

Living next to a volcano does have its benefits. The soil on Hawai'i is fertile and perfect for growing crops. Also, because of Hawai'i's mild climate, people can grow crops all year round.

a lava flow at Hawai'i Volcanoes National Park

6 How do people live in the wettest places?

Mawsynram, India, is the wettest place on the planet. The average rainfall is about 11,800 millimetres a year.

Mawsynram has a long **monsoon** season. June, July and August are the wettest months.

children shelter under a knup

People stay dry using umbrella shields called knups, which are made from plants. It is too wet for farming, so food is brought in from drier areas and sold in covered markets.

Because normal building materials would rot away in the rain, people use the roots of the trees to build bridges. They are woven across bamboo structures to form a living bridge.

Fact!
The oldest known "living bridges" are said to be over 500 years old.

Living in the Amazon

The Amazon rainforest is known for its heat, rain and more rain!

It's estimated there are around 400–500 **tribes** living here. About 50 of these tribes have never had contact with the outside world. They are well adapted to life in the rainforest.

Some tribes live a nomadic lifestyle. They settle in small villages for four to five years until the resources are used up. They then move on to another area, leaving the rainforest to recover. Why do you think they do this?

Whole areas of the Amazon can be flooded for six months of the year. People build tall wooden houses so they can live above the floodwaters. All the buildings are on stilts, even the chicken coops. People get around using boats.

7 The driest places

The Atacama Desert, in northern Chile and southern Peru, is one of the driest places on the planet.
The desert is about 2,500 metres above sea level which makes it the highest desert in the world. The average rainfall is about 15 millimetres a year, although some areas receive as little as one to three millimetres a year.

Most towns are located along the coast for fishing. There are some inland towns and villages, but these are found next to **oases**.

Because of its high **altitude**, little cloud cover and almost zero light pollution, the desert is one of the best places in the world for astronomy.

How many stars can you see at night? Do you ever see this change, depending on where you are looking at the sky?

Where do you think the driest place is?

You may not think it, but Antarctica is the driest continent on Earth. It is almost entirely desert. It hardly ever snows or rains there and, because it's so cold, the rain and snow that does fall doesn't melt.

Antarctica attracts people from across the world. 30 different countries have 80 research stations here. The population of researchers and scientists can reach around 4,000 residents. They share Antarctica with around 12 million penguins.

Antarctica is a tough place to live, even temporarily. As well as being very cold, it also has some of the highest wind speeds ever recorded.

How could you protect yourself against these temperatures?

Fact!

Scientists have recorded gusts of wind travelling at 321 kilometres per hour.

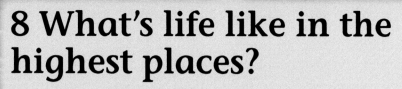

8 What's life like in the highest places?

The highest town in the world is La Rinconada, Peru. It is almost 5,000 metres above sea level. The town spends much of the year in sub-zero temperatures.

The air is very thin. Each breath contains half the amount of **oxygen** as at sea level. Despite this, over 50,000 people chose to live here for its famous gold mines.

People who visit high altitudes may find it difficult to breathe because of the thin air. Those who live there have evolved to cope with low oxygen levels.

Some runners train at high altitudes. Why do you think they do this? Their lungs slowly build more capacity over time in the higher altitudes.

Fact!
More than 140 million people worldwide live higher than 2,500 metres above sea level.

9 The lowest places

The lowest point on dry land is the shore of the Dead Sea.

No fish live in the sea as it is too salty. The water contains ten times more salt than ordinary seawater. In fact, the water is so salty, you can float on the top with no effort.

Fact!

The shores of the Dead Sea are 432.65 metres below sea level.

Bangladesh is a low-lying country which floods every year. It is covered by more than 230 rivers. How do you think they stop buildings from washing away?

Some houses are built on two-metre-high concrete stilts, which can stand against floods and **cyclone** winds of up to 241 kilometres per hour.

People created floating gardens to grow crops even when their farming fields are covered in flood water. In some areas, the water had become too salty to grow rice, so farmers began to farm shrimp.

10 Interesting places

Are you afraid of heights? Korowai people have been building their towering treehouses in the Indonesian Rainforest, New Guinea, for thousands of years.

These are floating villages in Tonle Sap, Cambodia. Most of the wooden homes are tied to bamboo rafts that float on the surface of the great lake.

The Hanging Temple near Datong, China, was built 75 metres above ground over 1,500 years ago. It was built to avoid floods, and the mountain shields it from heavy rain and snow.

Fact!

Ao-shima is an island close to Japan. It is nicknamed "Cat Island" and with good reason.

Only 20 people live on this island, but they share it with over 120 cats!

All over the globe, people survive, and thrive, in extreme climates. From the hottest to the coldest, the highest to the lowest, people living in very different places often have a lot in common.

They have found clever and sometimes surprising ways to find food and shelter, to be comfortable and to have fun!

Glossary

altitude height of a place above sea level

crops plants people grow to be eaten or sold

cyclone a tropical storm

geysers hot springs which can send water shooting into the air

herders people who look after groups of animals

inhabited lived in

monsoon a time of heavy rain

nomadic moving from place to place

oases areas of desert where water is found

oxygen an invisible gas in the air that we breathe

remote a place that is far away from anything else

tribes groups of people

tundra a large treeless and frozen area

Index

Where would you live?

Utqiagvik

Reykjavik

NORTH

Chicago

Death Valley AMERICA

Hawaii

La Rinconada SOUTH
AMERICA

Oymyakon

Rjukan

ROPE

Ulaanbaatar

ASIA Xuankong Si

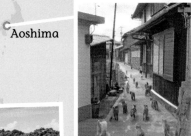

Aoshima

Doha Mawsynram

Bangladesh

Dallol

AFRICA

Coober Pedy OCEANIA

47

Ideas for reading

Written by Christine Whitney

Primary Literacy Consultant

Reading objectives:

- be introduced to non-fiction books that are structured in different ways
- listen to, discuss and express views about non-fiction
- retrieve and record information from non-fiction
- discuss and clarify the meanings of words

Spoken language objectives:

- participate in discussion
- speculate, hypothesise, imagine and explore ideas through talk
- ask relevant questions

Curriculum links: Geography: Physical geography; Writing: Write for different purposes

Word count: 2636

Interest words: extreme, altitude, inhabit, adapt, nomadic

Resources: paper, pencils and crayons, resources to make a simple rain or wind gauge

Build a context for reading

- Ask the group to discuss times when the weather has been very hot, very cold or very wet.
- Encourage children to look closely at the front cover of the book. Ask for a volunteer to explain what the word *extreme* means and how it relates to the photograph on the cover.
- Read the blurb on the back cover. Does anyone know of any *communities* or people that live in extreme places?

Understand and apply reading strategies

- Read the contents page and ask children to choose the chapter they are most interested in reading about. Ask them to share why this is so.
- Read Chapter 2 together. Ask children to explain how *some cities have gone to extreme lengths to keep people protected during the cold winters.*